PRETEND YOU DON'T KNOW ME

Finuala Dowling was born in Cape Town, South Africa in 1962, the seventh child in a family of eight. She started to write poetry only once she turned 40, but has since become one of her country's most popular poets and novelists. Her fourth novel, *The Fetch*, won the 2016 Herman Charles Bosman prize and was described by reviewer Dineke Volschenk as a book that 'in years to come, will bear testimony to the maturity and intelligence of South African culture and literature'.

She divides her time between writing and her role as senior lecturer in the Centre for Extra-Mural Studies at the University of Cape Town, where she is part of a team that organises its annual Summer School. She lives in the seaside town of Muizenberg with her sister Cara. She has a daughter, Beatrice, who also writes poetry.

Her first book-length UK publication, *Pretend You Don't Know Me: New and Selected Poems*, was published by Bloodaxe in 2018.

FINUALA DOWLING

Pretend You Don't Know Me

NEW AND SELECTED POEMS

BLOODAXE BOOKS

ISBN: 978 1 78037 424 6

First published 2018 by
Bloodaxe Books Ltd,
Eastburn,
South Park,
Hexham,
Northumberland NE46 1BS.

www.bloodaxebooks.com
For further information about Bloodaxe titles
please visit our website or write to
the above address for a catalogue.

Supported using public funding by
**ARTS COUNCIL
ENGLAND**

Cover design: Neil Astley & Pamela Robertson-Pearce.

Printed in Great Britain by Bell & Bain Limited, Glasgow, Scotland, on
acid-free paper sourced from mills with FSC chain of custody certification.

CONTENTS

from I FLYING (2002)

11 Green house
12 I read the last page first
14 Repair
15 For Oom Piet
16 I flying
17 To the doctor who treated the raped baby
    and who felt such despair
18 Census man
20 I have been undemonstrative since birth
21 Nine kinds of silence
22 Teaching Margaret Atwood
24 Kitchen table
26 The idea of you
27 Rule three thousand and ten
28 Fine in the Transkei
29 Blackjack
30 Under anaesthetic
32 Happy New Year 2001
34 Found poem

from DOO-WOP GIRLS OF THE UNIVERSE (2006)

39 Feeling marginalia
40 Talk, share and listen
41 Freelance writer's lament
42 Last straw
43 The differences between Middle and Modern English
45 Well
46 Disappearing

47   Asylum

48   My sister's fingers

49   Boys we kissed

50   The falling feeling

51   On the roof with Rory, 1976

53   Loving novels

55   Shops of my mother's imagination

56   Your death

57   The lime-green clasp

59   Doo-wop girls of the universe

from **NOTES FROM THE DEMENTIA WARD** (2008)

63   Your children, parents, siblings, spouses, pets, bêtes noires, acquaintances

64   At eight-five, my mother's mind

65   Taking

66   Lastness

67   Shift aside

68   Be shared

69   Self-portrait from the dementia ward

70   Hearts of stone

71   Widowhood in the dementia ward

72   Butter

73   An initiative to increase the number of male readers

74   Brief fling in the dementia ward

75   Multilingualism in the dementia ward

76   Odd one out in the dementia ward

77   More advanced thinking in the dementia ward

78   Devolution in the dementia ward

79   Protection from grief in the dementia ward

80   Red rover

81   Birthday in the dementia ward

82   How I knew it wasn't me

83   Homesickness

84   Riches

85   Bread roll pun

86   Thoughts on emigration

87   How to use a porcupine as an alibi

89   I am the zebra

91   Summarising life

from CHANGE IS POSSIBLE (2014)

95   Micheál Mac Liammóir came to Cape Town in 1962

96   Ditty

97   Caveat

98   Wanting to get divorced #1365

99   How sweet the dead are now

100   I gossip with my sister about the future

101   On not liking oneself

102   The consolation of enmity

103   The quest

104   To adventurers, as far as I'm concerned

105   Mise-en-abyme

106   Cupboards

107   Authority

108   Composition

109   The abuse of cauliflowers

110   The lawmaker

from NEW POEMS

112   Casting the cat and the bull

114   Unforgettable

115   Life lesson

116   To young women, urging them not to become competent

117   To my sisters, on selling the old family home

118   My therapist asks when it is that I cry

119   Dog produces Monet forgery

120   Catch of the day

121   Identity crisis 2016

122   Distant mirror

123   It's only lunch

124   The problem with this game drawn out in chalk

125   My mother the crocodile-tamer

126   Party invitations

127   Why I love an insult

128   Unhappiness

129   Two bodies could not be less alike than ours

130   One in a million

131   When panicking, think of the recently dead

132   Doubt

133   Ilk

134   How a house feels when we leave

136   ACKNOWLEDGEMENTS

FROM

I flying

(2002)

Green house

I live in a large green house
with my daughter and three dogs.
Also here you may find sister,
certainly brother,
and mother (grand).

No husband,
and no cat.

People sometimes ask about the cat.

I read the last page first

I read the last page first.
That's my confession:
I know the worst –
I read the last page first.

When I was a child
we drove in the dark past a neon sign
for the cocktail bar
at the Balmoral Hotel:
pretty pink lips
touching a glass of champagne
and I thought
that's it – that's Life –
take me there.

That page was the first.
That's when and how
I developed the thirst.
But now I read the last page first.

I married a man
who said he'd always loved that neon sign
yearned to be a bubble on those pink lips
when he was a boy driven past
the knocked down, no more
Balmoral Hotel
and I thought
this is it – this is Life –
I am here.
That page was the first.
A poignant tale, that's why
my bubble burst.
But now I read the last page first.

I stood in the aisle
of Shoprite Checkers with ghostly pink lips
and a man with a foreign accent said,
Excuse me are you married?
As if this were still the ladies bar
of the Balmoral Hotel.
And I said
this is not a bar –
read the sign.

Repair

Two friends of mine, hardly blood brothers,
have this in common: that they lost their mothers
to heaven or a better man at the tender age of four –
the same age as Beatrice when they met us.
Like all my friends they brought her treats,
teased her sweetly or applauded her feats
so that I thought, how good – they are healed –
they are here with us grown ups on the other side.
Until I noticed how when Beatrice cried
the great racking sobs of a child who is tired,
or defeated, or strung out like straining wire,
these friends followed when I carried her to bed,
stayed for the story, the caressing of the head,
waited for the bottle, the curtains drawn across
on a room full of children and their irreparable loss.

For Oom Piet

When I was least happy in life
my daughter led me across the road
to a neighbour whom I did not know
with the purpose of a toddler
who does not see gates and fences
but the ducks and puppies
on the other side

You spoke to me in the same low murmuring tones
you used for lame horses and bilious dogs.
Crops, flowers and poultry were our theme:
you made me tea and wiped the counter,
you said '*Foeitog*' and 'I don't hope so.'
You guessed.
You told me I was beautiful,
in the courtly way of an old man.

One day when it rained
you phoned from your side and said
'I'm sending some ducks for Beatrix'
– you always called her 'Beatrix' –
out the window we saw them,
waddling over,
in the way of ducks
when directed by Oom Piet.

You moved and I moved, but one thing stays:
the sense of a rescue, somehow being saved.

I flying

We were the flotsam of the day,
last twisted remnants of the brutal cold,
bent on a wind-wrecked, kelp-jet beach
with the baby Gabriel in tow.
The mad-cap girls rolled the pram
till it sped like tossed foam, though,
long-legged, the pilot boy still strolled.

Pressing for a salt-wounded shore,
I was drenched in this sense of
   I can't take much more
when I saw your arms stretch wide
from your chariot sides, and you cried:
'I flying.' 'I flying.' Oh Gabriel, only one,
the only one with wings – smile of 'behold!' –
for the storm-shattered, star-struck, fold.

To the doctor who treated the raped baby and who felt such despair

I just wanted to say on behalf of us all
that on the night in question
there was a light on in the hall
for a nervous little sleeper
and when the bleeding baby was admitted to your care
faraway a Karoo shepherd crooned a *ramkietjie* lullaby in the veld
and while you staunched
there was space on a mother-warmed sheet
for a night walker
and when you administered an infant-sized opiate
there were luxuriant dark nipples
for fist-clenching babes
and when you called for more blood
a bleary-eyed uncle got up to make a feed
and while you stitched
there was another chapter of a favourite story
and while you cleaned
a grandpa's thin legs walked up and down for a colicky crier
and when finally you stood exhausted at the end of her cot
and asked, 'Where is God?',
a father sat watch.
And for the rest of us, we all slept in trust
that you would do what you did,
that you could do what you did.
We slept in trust that you lived.

Census man

The census man came to count us. His bottom sank through the *riem*
of an old family chair. I am here, he said, as I looked at him,
his pencil poised in the air, I am here, in the year 2001
to count your mother's children (every one)
and to find out the nature of their business
and who is their God
and if they still know or notice
whether they're black or white or Indian.

Your mother's name?
Eve, I replied.
Please bear in mind, ladies and gentlemen
he was here to count all of all of all of all of
our mother's children.

The head of this household is white and female
born in 1921, Ficksburg, OFS.
With a diploma in drama and elocution
and 8 live births to her credit.
Her status is widow and she earns
R500 per month. The head of this household
has no serious disabilities other than a feeling
of immobility and not knowing where she's put her glasses.

Oh Mr Census man, don't you want to know
that my mother loves the sun, loves her children every one?
And the farms she's never owned, and the dark mystique of Rome?
And her brain has solved the cyphers of all your wars?

The nature of her business, said the census man
is live births, 8 live births.
I'll put it on the form and I'll tell all the earth
about 8 live births.

Ma sat in the yard on an old plastic chair
and the last rays of autumn caught her silver hair.
Beaty came running, 'Granny!' she said, 'there's
a man here with mummy and I think we've done
something wrong, but he's giving us a second chance'.

But Ma was on a tangent that starts with imperial decrees
sent from Caesar in Rome and goes on through second Eves
and live births in Bethlehem taking us straight to the Free State
and the old days in Ficksburg where the sun beats down, lonely,
on a little Basuto pony.

I have been undemonstrative since birth

But interestingly, I have always hugged babies
especially if they are related to me
and once I kissed a friend with positive HIV
so it is true but not completely that
I have been undemonstrative since birth.

And also I found that at an evangelical ceremony
when the spirit entered those around me
My arms were lifted up spontaneously
arousing great familial mirth.
Thus it is true but not completely that
I have been undemonstrative since birth.

At Mandela's inauguration I remember too
the ululating women who shared my food
and who, because we were happy then, completely,
made me dance, all swept up in their girth:
a small white woman of great reserve
who has been undemonstrative since birth.

Nine kinds of silence

I have mouthed the muting of acute physical pain.
I have committed the silence of obdurateness.
I have overcome the winded, wounded heart-stop of taken breath.
I have left my body behind in waiting-room stillness.
I am familiar with the can't-get-a-word-in-edgewise pause.
I am a veteran of bored deadening.
I have relished the gull's distant cry of a lull.
I have taken notes in quiet communion with myself.

    I am silent.

        Except if specifically requested to speak,
           or if I have more than two glasses of wine at a party.
    Then I am quite hilarious and men fall in love with me
and women ask if we can meet for breakfast or tea.

Afterwards, stifling shame, I spin again my soft cocoon and sleep,
fleeced in the nine kinds of silence you know me by: Nu.

Teaching Margaret Atwood

Most meaning comes as a vista,
a sudden access of plain and space.
And joy, I forgot, sheer happiness.
But when we read her poem, the class
saw nothing, nothing opened.
Why did the speaker (in the poem)
want a corner of sunlight to lie in?
Why did (she) want a sunny room?
And find no room, and find no sun?
The poem was bad, self-pitying.

I remembered myself at nineteen,
locked out, virginal, unbereaved,
reading 'Lycidas' with an old HB
which splintered softly in my mouth.
Bent over the blue-mantled shepherd,
(who did not really batten his flocks
but something else: the human spirit
against loss), I recognised what poets do:
stand on the rise and call: 'Weep no more',
impatiently, when the tide is out, and
the reborn sun setting on the floodless plain.
I was slow, coming after to the view,
but still I felt his cloak brush past my cheek,
and held within me these words as true:
'Tomorrow to fresh woods, and pastures new.'

Here is tomorrow and these woods are old
and known. I have been the one curled up,
twisting towards corners and shafts of sun.
I know the dread of space; I have lain down
on the 'pissed floor' till I could weep no more.

So, now I understand your meaning and it comes
not as a vista, nor is it plain. There is no rise here,
no place to stand and view. I am completely
unconsoled. Your mantle is a jacket, tied and strait.
This is my own old home, cold and roomless
that you have brought me to. At last,
I look out. Faces watch me, nineteen and lost,
but trusting me to trace, with pencil soft,
a sunset, dot-to-dot.

Kitchen Table

Breadcrumbs of my childhood are wedged
here in the puttied grooves of this table
of my forebears. Near an Aga stove it stood
and my Bisto nose just reached its level
as a bustling nanny brought a hot black pan
of fat for a bread feast. We were not poor.
Underneath you could sit on the struts
and move the drawers above like a private
car or a machine of your imagination until
you were coaxed out to have your cradle cap
brushed into the slow floating snow storm
of a European picture book. This table too
has been the station of every departure and
every return, the journey of growing up that
began with the maid who said, 'Tie your own
laces,' and continued through the death of my
father, signalled by the angle of my mother's
hand on the kettle as I ran in from catechism,
and followed by the long black tunnel of
uncertain finances from which we emerged
sanded down and gleaming with promise.

The table transformed into a chopping block
where my mother decapitated all traitors and
heartbreakers with her onion knife and we
laughed at a moist wedding cake fallen and
filled with gravel, and at visitors who said
'I don't mind if I do'. I drank coffee desperately
holding onto its hard edges after late nights
drinking with a boy who said, 'Hey, fuck,
Finuala, I only dig your fridge,' and helped
himself to a turkey leg. His head rolled. After

the revolution, I continued to send letters home,
unfolded here among the Marmite and the
honeyed ants, until I too was stamped and sent
back to its four-square strength. There is a queue
for the thin chair near the toaster. I sit there on a
pile of unironed laundry, blocking the door jamb,
thinking about the bread and crumbs of all my life
and tears of laughter shed by the onion knife.

The idea of you

I thought I'd always love
fat men, loud men, flamboyant men,
useless men, molly-coddled men, lazy men,
cheating men, material men, gimme men:
Men like shopping malls.

I've always liked vegetarian men,
fussy men, mean men, demanding men,
angry men, know-it-all men, men-in-therapy,
look-at-me men, childless men:
Men like problem pages.

But all the time I was loving them,
before I'd even met you,
I was longing for you (the idea of you)
as one longs for pillow and sheet.

A man as calm as a beach walk,
as rangy as a cowboy and his lasso,
a man with livestock and hills
and a river with fish, and a racing bike,
whose heart still runs free
down some farm road of his infancy;
who fixes things and reads and sings
and doesn't want to hear anything
but my voice in a shell and
doesn't want to hurt anyone
but my enemies (the idea of them),
or keep anything
except the idea of me.

Rule three thousand and ten

I've forgotten a lot of the rules,
like how you get to the square on the hypotenuse,
(and what to wear once you're there)
and how to do long division,
and getting percentages on a calculator.
Netball draws a blank.
Don't even know the right way to lace shoes,
or the bowl to use when whipping chocolate mousse.
Why one is not supposed to clink glasses,
or say 'Pleased to meet you'.
What to say when someone dies,
or to do if they do.
And when to say 'owing' and when to say 'due'
(not that I ever have good reason to).
What has gone away?
The whole thing about the past tense in French novels.
The meaning of zig zag yellow road markings.
The rite of contrition after confession.

But I'll always remember rule three thousand and ten:
never sleep with married men.

Fine in the Transkei

I was fine in the Transkei, I
rode the potholed road, oh
I eyed the blanketed old oh
I smiled an oyster smile, I
dote on bloat black swine, I
I slide on wine, oh float on boat,
and swam to mangrove island, man.

Not bored in the Transkei, I
stored a general store, nor
warred when white men swore or
saved a craven slave; I
climbed the windy hill till
chill cling in my sides, I
note unstolen phone, oh.

Till rising tide arrive I
sigh to be alive I
silver through the blue. You
saw the full moon too, you
warmed the meeting sheets, you
knife the dying cray-day, I
hold my fears at bay.

Pairs lay and kissed who
missed the passing kiss too
much to hit the clicks or catch
the thatchers thatch or
walk through cows, not flowers –
Though all those hours were ours.
I was fine in the Transkei, aye.

Blackjack

blackjack n. The spiky, adhesive seed of the weed *Bidens pilosa* which clings firmly.

He loved her words which caught
him so much like blackjacks
that he wanted to undress
her because she seemed such
an attractive person and so
different from his wife.
He wooed and wooed with
all his exercise till she
succumbed in a bed of
country veld where
blackjacks hooked onto
her unwanted underwear and
that was very nice but
he missed her words and
her body was as smooth as
his wife's. So very tenderly
he removed from her sweater
the blackjacks one by one and
sent her back to her writing
board where she pinned
her blanket-stabber weeds
one by one and bit
back the cat-yowl sting.

Under Anaesthetic

I woke up and heard
them hacking and yabbering
and jawing and sawing
off some real bone of
mine to replace it with
a prosthesis to which
I must have consented.

It was an all-male team,
the chain-saw gang.
The chief surgeon, in the
airline flaps, who had least
liked my hips (or was it my
stocking tops?), hence the
blindfold eyes, was my ex.
He was moving his lips
to keep his mind off the
blood, which always made him
sick. Among others at the
task in their respective
masks, I recognised one who'd
always slaughtered his own
meat and so should not have
balked to see me on the block.

But you know, once they get
to the caucus on which cuts to
take and which not, it's pretty
much over and you're a
carcass anyway. Of course
when I came round again, though
I was not myself, I said: 'I was

awake, I heard it all, every last
syllable,' and they replied
'You're wrong, it's quite
impossible.' To which
I must have assented.

Happy New Year 2001

Down on earth
they are discussing the latest publishing sensation
and a brilliant movie made with Plasticine models.

I'm in orbit
that's why I can't join in but only, endlessly, overhear
howareyouhowareyouhowareyouhowareyouhowareyou?

Nobody's well
but everyone's fine. Though on the first day Kay noticed a dead
      body smell outside her door
& mentioned how a friend of hers can't sleep at night but listens
      to the boats
& on the second my daughter was caught crushing periwinkles in
      a marine sanctuary
& on the third Paul inherited a kind of urn from his dead mother
& yesterday Robin saw five shoals of yellowtail in the depleted bay
& in the last year generally little William's been banned from TV
      for slow speech development
& no one benefited from apartheid so no one will sign the pledge
& Cara says a boy we knew who was fed on a diet of religion has
      been drinking his clients' money
& his sister lost two babies at the breast & their brother died of a
      punctured lung
& Guy hears that Christopher who has beautiful legs ate Provita
      for his Xmas lunch
& the otherwise talented boy won't or can't come out of the
      bathroom
& similarly an actress we know went out to buy cigarettes but
      didn't come back
& a bookcase crashed down on our empty guest bed proving says
      my mother that novels can kill

& Noelle doesn't want any more muffins & may have to have her
   foot amputated
& Manuel says that the League of the Friends of the Blind feeds
   him dog food
& Ida the bergie's uncle says Cape Town's no place for her
& she must take the six children out of welfare & come to Zim in
   his Continental
& Mary who was incontinent at night but otherwise in good
   spirits finally went like a bride of Christ
& Lynda in a doubtful fur coat spoke to a man who'd been in
   solitary in the eastern bloc
& her sister says when you visit Robben Island you get barked at
   & herded like in the old regime
& someone threw up on the ferry & my neighbour shouts at her
   seven-year old even when he's quiet
& eight Fridays ago someone abandoned my heart in cold empty
   space
& I've gone into orbit but thank you I am fine
& yes I'm sure the film is brilliant
& the book is sensational
& I'll certainly get around to them.

Found poem

When asked by concerned parties
whether I've submitted
any creative writing lately, you know, rhymes
I want to scream & scream,
Where Do You Think I Would Find the Time?
Every moment I have is mortgaged
off another moment.
If I go for a walk I fall behind,
I fall behind and I mind falling behind
with the marking. Or at two in the afternoon,
poised on the brink
poised on the brink of a thought
a child interrupts

a lesson a lecture a sonnet a thread
shreds itself in my cheese-grater head
to be collected and recollected later,
in a time slot allotted for something unrelated.

I'm saving time as it is by not speaking,
by living in this intertidal zone
where communication washes over me,
friends twinkle distantly on rocky, dangerous
promontories I no longer approach.

Or I crash into them
in supermarkets, me picking
up the groceries between domestic duties
& study guides & yes! – ha! I catch laughing couples
opening litres of cooldrink in the juice aisle,
droëbek from last night's party – up late & dancing,
& another one coming, & I speaking to them,

it feels like, through sheets of one way glass
& they ask, have you written anything lately,
you know, creatively, & I just shake my head
& think: You hedonists! layabouts! slugabeds!
Where Do You Think I Would Find The Time?

But I stop & I think:
I should live
I should sing the blues
should party all night & then swig unpaid-for juice
in the aisles of Pick 'n Pay
in the new Long Beach Mall
till the deadlines whizz by, & say
to my employers, fuck you all
& write poems in lipstick
& stick them in bottles
for my *babbalas* friends
to get stuck in their throttles
& I will do just this,
when I find the time.

FROM

Doo-Wop Girls of the Universe

(2006)

Feeling marginalia

My daughter marks my work:
'Good work, Jane!' Or Chelsea,
Rose or Jade.
I get eight out of ten
or even full marks with a red pen.
She finds my notes for books and lectures
in the recycle bin, takes them
to her room and marks them,
always very generously,
the teacher I would have loved
to have. Sometimes when
I am working back to back,
day to night without pause,
she comes to my study
looking for her mother.
She waits on the visitor's chair.
Then, when I do not see her,
she takes the sidelined pages
that once had my full attention
and marks them all with feeling
marginalia. 'Good!' she calls me,
'Excellent!' –
when I am not.

Talk, share and listen

I was meant to be writing a poem
but because I'm human I made a lasagne instead
while simultaneously composing a poem in my head
and thinking about an article I'd read, which said
poets on average live for only 62.2 years.
(It is Ferlinghetti's fault, I think, that we look so long-lived.
Born 1919 and still going – he may make a hundred.)
You can tell if a poet's depressed, say researchers,
because we write more 'I's' and more 'me's' and choose
fewer words of rapport such as 'talk', 'share' and 'listen'.

Ho, hmm, talk, share and listen.

In fact I made two lasagnes, since some people like meat
whereas others won't eat things which once had feet.
I was cooking to escape my screen. On it were two lines:
Poets end their own lives
But politicians have to be shot.
How dreadful. I said that. I wish I had not.

Ho, hmm, talk, share and listen.

There is an art to making lasagne while simultaneously
composing a poem. Lasagnes are quite complicated
and deep. They come in layers with blank sheets
in between. Lasagnes are best assembled alone,
in a serious and contemplative atmosphere, and should,
wherever possible, be allowed to stand quite long
before being read aloud to create a frisson
at occasions where one gathers to talk, share and listen.

Freelance writer's lament

The man in the van with glass panes trussed to the sides
knows what he has to do
The bricklayer donning his hard hat
knows what he has to do
The clerk in a headscarf waiting for the Post Office to open
knows what she has to do
The labourer cycling along the country road
knows what has to do
The blue-checked chef with fresh ingredients
knows what he has to do
The woman unlocking the iron grille of her shop
knows what she has to do.

But I might do anything today.

I could write twenty wonderful pages
or nothing at all
I could finish four commissions
or stare at the wall
I could answer every single mail
or wait for the call
I could parcel up manuscripts with brown paper and string
or crumple here, like a damn frayed knot, 'fraid not.
I might be a writer
or I might be a paper ball.

Last straw

On this day when I wake at five
in order to launder and to write
before serving tea and rusks
and packing lunch, finding socks,
then stuck in slow traffic, gouging
my heart out for five hours to yawns
or jocular resistance, before returning
via the shops to answer mail
and phone calls; fetching, feeding,
empathising and in turn offloading,
about the horror of marking, preparing,
and supervising, I pray like a camel
who has counted every straw, every leaf:
Let no-one die, or even graze their knee.

The differences between Middle and Modern English

So suddenly in Middle English
we start to sound like ourselves.
'Why did they call their language
Middle English?' queries Stacey.
No, we called it that, we name
everything for our convenience.

Now, after 1066, we – gradually –
lost inflections, word endings,
like the -ed in 'She loved Sushi'.
'Oh I do too,' says Annaelle, 'sushi is
my best.' Good, I say, Now: in the days of
Alfred, we had a lot more. Not sushi,
no. 'Aren't you cold?' Aimee asks Chris,
who is proudly showing his new tattoo.

Today, our poor bare nouns and poorly
dressed verbs are committed to SVO.
Subject Verb Object. 'I love Sushi', not
'Sushi loved I' . 'I loved the man' not
'The man I loved' – that's a fragment,
a mere noun phrase, which we are not
doing today, the full sentence of which
would be, say 'The man I loved *left* me',
where 'loved' is weak, but 'left' is strong,
going tightly into the past by itself.
Leave – left. Weep – wept.

           You will also notice
that Chaucer's pronouns are closer
to ours. A pronoun is a word that stands
in for you when you are not around.

We all need pronouns. Persons
are singular or plural. *He* loved her;
She loved him. Singular. Sadly,
they were divorced. Plural.
'Ag shame,' says Stacey, 'who?' No, no
it's just an example. 'Sorry,' says Stacey.

Moving on, then, the French of course,
brought thousands of words – 'beef' for 'cow',
'judgement' for 'doom' and 'desire' for 'wish'.
'They're not the same,' said Aimee,
'desire and wish.' Quite right, I say,
and in the shadow and the shortfall
of this subtle difference – desire and wish –
lies our English.

Well

When I am down my well,
the one with slippery black sides,
no toeholes, and only a pinhole
of light 3000 compass turns above,
I still describe myself as 'fine'.

I am thinking of saying 'well'
instead. Yes, I think in future
I will definitely reply, 'I am well'.

'Well' is more accurate,
and more of a cry for help.

Disappearing

It's nearly evening
the fan is whirring

people have been calling me 'she' all day.

If I wait here all night –
keep a disappearing vigil –
will I hear a gentle 'you'
before dawn?

Asylum

My family is a hospital
where the doctors and patients
are blood relatives,
and when you are not on call
you may lie down.

My sister's fingers

You should see my sister Cara dance
with these long practical fingers of hers
that act out the song and point the direction
you could go in if you could only hear the beat.
She uses them (fingers) in non-party situations too,
to say: 'Don't mess with me,' and also: 'Fuck you
Buck Rogers,' whatever that means (but it's mean,
I know). These fingers of sister Cara's, they're like
Moses' rod. She points them: the sea parts, the rock
opens, everyone leaves Egypt, gets enough to eat,
hears the rules.

       Now here is the news – she suffered
a minor stroke on election day in '94 –
our first free democratic vote. One of her famous
autocratic forefingers was struck down then, for good.

Boys we kissed

Our lips made history: boys we kissed
at seventeen are now distinguished men.
Old Mutual would fall without them.

They were divine, the boys we kissed.
Now call for stronger coffee, and more wine

Speechless then and staring, boys we kissed
became their betters, listed men of letters.
Public voices would not exist, but that we kissed.

They were divine, the boys we kissed.
Now call for stronger coffee, and more wine

History has dismissed who would not kiss us.
Down this southern strip, striplings hung on our lips:
we recast them as rock stars, as Swedish artists.
They are divine, the boys we kissed.

Now if only we could be heard above their noise
We'd call for stronger coffee and more boys.

The falling feeling

I came to our first meeting
with a falling feeling,
feeling of falling and fleeing.
Meeting you deeply on the way
down you said, 'I don't want to say
I'm falling in love with you.'
I said, 'Oh do, please, do do do.'
So you said it, oh you said it,
so deeply and it sounded true:
'I'm falling in love with you.'

I came to our first meeting
with a deeply falling feeling,
but I think you just caught me
reeling. You just reeled me in.

On the roof with Rory, 1976

We sat among the roofs
as if this were Cairo, not Kalk Bay.
Your mother's garden roof,
your mother's watercolour view:
the coloured quarter,
blue-tinct water,
edges indistinct.

I wanted your mother's life.
Even the wine's cold clay jug that hid
its lack of provenance or vintage.
Especially her kaftans – rows of them
(you showed me once): floating fabric
for a girl of fourteen's feelings.
Then her friends – their hooped earrings,
their political subterfuge,
their unlikely sexual permutations (one couple
had to be separated by a doctor, you said),
their hysterical conversations,
their 'God!' 'Darling!' flamboyance.

And in my innocence,
I wanted you, the boy next to me on the ledge,
who was, at seventeen, impatient,
broad of shoulder,
narrow of waist
and an artist
effortlessly
fledged.

The last light of the west cast down the gully
from Clovelly, and the village chilled.
'When you are a writer,' you asked,
'What will you write about?' I looked out
over the roofs, closed tight on people's lives,
and knew there would be stings
before I learnt to prise the lid off things.
(I also thought, 'But books are set in England!')
'Write about this,' you said,
your hand spread over the retracted hamlet.
Then you took off.
I knew how long it would take me,
so much longer than you,
but now I'm here too.

Loving novels

Now that I've published prose, which as everyone knows
is better than poetry – well, more noteworthy,
this makes me an author – well, not really an author,
but a woman author – and a certain kind of journalist
wants to know really important things about me, like:
What is my favourite colour?
What perfume do I wear?
What are my three all-time favourite novels?

Oh God I love the sham beginnings of the genre itself –
Defoe and Smollett and dear Fanny's letters –
I love the way it segues into Jane Austen's impeccable voice;
I love George Eliot's mastery over *Middlemarch*;
dialectal sex in Wessex with Thomas Hardy;
Joyce going round about himself in Dublin;
Virginia loving 'life, London, this moment in June'
before handing over to the Americans.

Like you I love the crack of books
and the smell inside the spines of new ones
but also bound vellum volumes with golden letters,
marbled end papers, leafed-in silken tassles
and ex-libris woodcuts of the dead beloved.

I love books about bookshops, books about bibliophiles
who smuggled books and saved them from bonfires.

I love books in which the book itself is being written
and books in which a book itself is being read.

I cannot exclude any novel that has made me weep
Or keep an all-night vigil, or laugh aloud, or sigh

and say, 'I'm so relieved you thought to write
what I have only groped for in my sleep.'

But if it helps: my favourite colour is purple
and I rarely go out the door without a hint of Dior.

Shops of my mother's imagination

It is better to shop in the shops
of my mother's imagination
They stock things like Optrex
and Yardley's Misty Beige foundation
(discontinued) and long-handled
dustpans and a remedy called Lexan
and very lightweight parasols and a cut
of meat she swears is called a Boston butt
and plain white cartridge for writing real letters
and finger-small bananas which she still remembers
from a long lost love affair in Barbados, West Indies.

Your death

Let me tell you about your death.

Disregarding murder, drowning, suicide,
road accident, shark bite and veld fire
in your direct and unavoidable path,

you will die of old age.

At this time, in the general bracket of your advanced age,
You will lack eyesight
You will lack mobility
You will lack short-term memory
You will lack an ordered sense of what is happening
You will lack well-being
You will lack sexual viability
You will lack presence
You will lack a complete index of living friends.

But I will still want you alive.
I will still fear the feeling of missing you.

On the other hand,
if I am already dead
when you reach this oldest age,
fed up and the hell-in with the unfairness
of my own unwinding
(you know me)
I will come looking for you.
And Ah!
the greeting.

The lime-green clasp

In my swims these mornings there's a slender,
almost hunchbacked with slenderness,
woman in a lime green bikini
and matching bathing cap
swimming her thirty lengths
(different strokes, including breast-)
with speed and accuracy.

Afterwards she gets out
and, very dextrously,
using her towel as a tent,
strips off.

Little wringing wet things
drop below
while big airy dry things
plop on from above.

And every morning some or other man
usually fully clothed –
just moseying about,
just hands-in-pockets-interested-in-the-beach,
watches her, especially the bit where she
unclips the lime green bra fastening,
leaning forward to keep the tent
pitched.

Sometimes, just between
the slipping towel,
the dripping bra,
the dropping top,
one sees through the flap

(but not always)
a slope of small breast.

Halfway through the striptease,
some of the rest of us start to watch
the man watching the woman.
Our eyes go to her too, but mostly to him,
because he is not frankly staring,
only slyly corner-of-his-eyeing.

At a certain point, the whole beach,
every hearty morning splasher,
every rock-hopping-dog-walker,
every toddler-following mother,
is fixed fast on the clasp
of the lime-green bikini top,
and its unfastening.

At last we are released.
We swing free.

Doo-wop girls of the universe

I know something you don't know
About the women you know –
those makers of decisions
physicians, rhetoricians,
amiable stage technicians,
indignant politicians,
formidable statisticians,
quiet dieticians
and the non-icians too,
the lovely –ists:
the linguists,
lyricists,
artists,
activists.

Almost every woman I've ever known –
whether she be -ician or she be -ist –
has told me once or shown
she'd really come into her own as
a doo-wop girl.

So put her in the footlights,
put her at the backing mics,
right up there on the dais,
maybe slightly out of focus
while some man sings his opus,
the undisputed locus
of attention.

Then while the main man
belts out the main track
she'll be in the back

going like so –
shoulders, head and toes –
hips, chest, east, west.
Best way to describe her pose
is 'biding',
she's biding time on the sidelines
waiting for the best lines –
the reprise –
the one we're born cooing:
ooby shooby doo
right on cue.

Look, I'm known to generalise
but I'd like to emphasise
that every woman has inside
a doo-wop girl.

Give her the mic, Mike
or I'll call my sisters,
'cause I got sisters,
and I'll say: 'Sisters,
you hang up those rubber gloves
you freeze that chicken
you unplug that iron
you come with me
we be free
we be threeness
we be supremes
we be the unforced
force of fourness
not sad, not terse:
doo-wop girls of the universe.'

Notes from the Dementia Ward

(2008)

Your children, parents, siblings, spouses, pets, bêtes-noir, acquaintances

They will all die
but not in the right order

At eighty-five, my mother's mind

When she wanders from room to room
looking for someone who isn't there,

when she asks where we keep the spoons,
when she can't chew and spits out her food,

when her last dim light flickers with falling ash
and she exclaims: 'What a dismal end to a brilliant day!'

when she calls her regular laxative an astronaut,
when she can't hear words but fears sounds,

when she says: 'Don't go – I can't bear it when you go,'
or: 'Just run me off the cliff,'
or wants to know how many Disprin ends it,

then I think how at eighty-five
my mother's mind is a castle in ruin.

Time has raised her drawbridge, lopped her bastions.
Her balustrade is crumbled, and she leans.

Yet still you may walk these ramparts in awe.
Sometimes when she speaks, the ghostly ensign flies.

Time cannot hide what once stood here,
or its glory.

Do not think that we are good
or merely tourists.

That which detains us
was once our fortress.

Taking

After two years of house arrest –
what they call 'home care' –
I take the soiled sheets from my sister,
put them in the machine,
lift the heavy carpet,
break down.

The men come running,
take the carpet from me
(something to do).

Then I steady my mad mother
who, staggering downstairs in her frail bones
and failing sight,
takes me in her arms and asks:
'What is the matter darling?
Whatever is the matter?'

Lastness

All this brouhaha about birthdays and first days
while anniversaries of lastness pass us by.

Hallmark has nothing to say about
the last time you laced your daughter's shoe,
the last time a stranger looked twice at your face,
the last time you swam naked,
the last time you ran so fast your chest burned,
the last time you made love and meant it.

Even if by carrot juice and determined zest
you have missed these listed lastnesses –
making meaningful naked underwater love
after lacing your surprised daughter's shoes –

you'll never avoid them all. In particular,
there will be a last day when you steer
your mad mother down her own front steps,
drive her silently from her own house
for the last time, carefully not saying:
'Look back, Ma, look up – that was your home.
You are seeing and leaving it for the last time.'

Carefully not saying:
'Because you no longer lace shoes.'

Shift aside

Those nights I lay awake, calculating our ages:
I was ten to your fifty,
    would be fifteen to your fifty-five,
        twenty to your sixty.

I pushed them as far as they would go:
    thirty to seventy,
        forty to eighty,
           fifty to ninety.
              The numbers toppled –
an orphan, at any age.

I stood in the dark doorway,
awaiting your invitation.
Sleepily, on your elbow,
you would ask: 'A nightmare?'
and shift aside on the three-quarter bed.

Your back was warm;
your pillow fragrant.

These nights I lie awake calculating our ages:
I am forty-five to your eighty-five,
    will be fifty to your ninety,
        sixty to your century.

I stand in a lit-up doorway
– disinfectant upon human soil.

You wince slightly as you shift aside,
pat the space beside you: 'Lie here.'

I wait only until you breathe evenly.

Be shared

Why can't you be more like
the new kitten
who creeps to Granny's bed
in the lonely afternoon
and sleeps there companionably
like an idling motor
that whirs into action
when Beaty with bells and strings
takes the stairs in twos
for fur and games;
nobody feeling faithless or betrayed?

Self-portrait from the dementia ward

After a few mouthfuls of supper
she lies back on her pillows,
struggling against the bedsore to be comfortable.

Words elude her: 'Everything is so...'
and she moves her elegant fingers
in a way to suggest a Jackson Pollock painting.

I think about prompting her
but I want to hear the substitute –
the synonym that her shattered genius will provide.

Even so I am surprised:
'...modernistic,' she says eventually
and closes her eyes,
exhausted by the last stand,
the self-portrait.

Hearts of stone

Downstairs my father drank gin and spun
If we only have love over and
over on the turntable –
he was immune to rehabilitation.

Upstairs my mother –
immune to Jacques Brel –
read to us from the great works of English Literature
and we wept for little Nell.

Widowhood in the dementia ward

'Oh my God, I'm so pleased to see you,'
she says from her nest of blankets.
'I've been meaning to ask –
How is your father?
How is Paddy?'

'He died,' I say, remembering 1974.

'Good heavens, now you tell me!
How lucky he is.'

'You could join him,' I suggest.

'I didn't like him *that* much,' she replies.

Butter

You know how it is sometimes with butter?
How after a free fallow period, you long for it,
how it lies shaded in its pale, soft firmness,
how it calls to you quietly from its cool clay dish

until at last you give in, you make toast:
you don't even want the toast –
burnt crumbs mean nothing to you –
but you but you but you want the butter.

Well, that's how it was with you.
I'm saying this in as plain a sliced way as I can –
there may after all be children present:
you were any old slice of toast.

I can't be more explicit than this;
I can't slick this on any thinner.
You may have thought you were the butter
but you weren't: you were the toast.

An initiative to increase the number of male readers

We do love men with charming looks
but send us more who have read books.

We ogle men who're built like champs
but send us more with reading lamps.

We still like men who make us passes
but send in more with reading glasses.

We'll race with men in racy cars
if they have valid library cards.

Please, please goddess, before it's bed
send in men who have read
hardbacks.

Brief fling in the dementia ward

My mother has a brief flirtation
with Mr Otto, a rare male in Frail Care.
He has the look of a Slavic conductor
– sweeping, side-parted silver locks
offset his visible nappy line.

'How odd,' Ma says of Mr Otto,
'to meet the love of one's life in a kitchen'
and to him, within hearing of the nurses:
'Your place or mine?'

But then, just as quickly, she forgets him
and Mr Otto wanders the passageways again,
asking if anyone has seen his wife;
it's not like Mrs Otto to be home so late.

Multilingualism in the dementia ward

When I release her from the restraining chair
she is grateful for her freedom
but concerned for the guest she is leaving behind:
'I'm so sorry, but we're leaving now.'

'Uh uh uh uh!' groans the trapped Alzheimer's patient.

With a lifetime's practice of politeness, my mother listens:
'I beg your pardon? Really? I must look into that.'

We walk out. I am humbled by her power:
'Do you understand the language that woman speaks?'

'Oh yes …
I *think* it's Sotho.'

Odd one out in the dementia ward

It's a cold, bleak day
which might explain why she says:
'This is my daughter Nuala,
who has come all the way from South Africa to visit me.'

'Though,' she adds, looking at the nurse,
'by the looks of you, you come from there too.'

Well satisfied with her own civility,
she whispers: 'I was going to say
This is my daughter Nuala –
she's just a *little* bit odd.'

More advanced thinking from the dementia ward

Like a mistrustful toddler
she keeps opening her eyes to check on me

because, as she says,
I have a habit of slipping away.

'I have to leave now, Ma – it's school tomorrow
and I've forgotten to turn up Beaty's winter skirt.'

'If you just concentrate hard enough,
the skirt will turn itself up.'

Devolution in the dementia ward

My mother's tongue is lizard-like now
as she devolves.

Still, she discriminates:
'This place is full of the most boring lunatics.'

Protection from grief in the dementia ward

Told about her son's funeral
she replies –
'I think you're mistaken,
you have the surname wrong'

How her madness growls
wards off grief

Red rover

(for Sean Dowling, 1953-2007)

Dear companion of our youth when we were immortal
and our happy shouts swung up through the gum trees,
when we raced go-carts in order to destroy our knees,
when there were always eight of us home for tea
and eight of us learning to count and read
and eight of us crammed into the Fiat for Mass
and eight of us slashing through the long dry grass
and four of you dive-bombing four of us
and all of us playing 'Red rover, red rover come over!'

You who knew so much about the love of homes,
returning often to those ruins, then sitting next to the toaster
saying: 'I've been back there, you know –
I've found the dogs' graves and a foundation stone.'

You're there now. You took a sickle to the long dry grass
and found our old home – the fastest to follow the call:
'Red rover, red rover, come over.'

Birthday in the dementia ward

We are discussing her eighty-sixth birthday.
She pulls herself up from her cushions:
'I wonder – I would really like my mother to come –
could you arrange that?'

(Your mother was born in 1888,
even if she were Japanese
she could not come.)

'I'll see if I can arrange transport.'

How I knew it wasn't me

I only realised I was at risk
when my brother phoned to check if I was still alive –

he'd heard it on the radio:
a woman fitting my description apparently wept
on the harbour wall before she dived.

      'So it wasn't you?'
a query rising in his tone.

I too – as I replied – couldn't help sounding
      unconvinced
as if searching for stronger proof.

After verbally confirming my existence,
I walked to the bay window and considered
the breakwater, the beacon
      the beckoning sea
and the woman who jumped in my place.

Homesickness

I know that no one will ever love me
so little as this hotel room
high-rise and franchised
it spits at me its
grudging sachets and tight sheets.

I know that no one will ever love me
so little or so anonymously
as the twin pictures of nothingness
on the wall of this hotel room
that doesn't love me
in so many ways –
with its flickering bathroom bulb,
tepid water,
detergent carpet
and deathtrap view of the freeway.

> Though once in a crowded dining room you begged:
> 'Pretend you don't know me' (and I didn't)
> still you loved me more than this hotel room.

This hotel room won't follow me into the night air
like an electrician familiar with my porcelain fuses
and this hotel room will never say: 'Sorry'
or hold me close and let me weep for home.

Riches

I have no money in the bank,
no immediate prospect of work.

I am driving home on the coastal road,
the most beautiful road in the world.

Almost everyone I love
lives in the blue clefts ahead.

Molten sun heats my right cheek;
evaporating sea cools my left.

I am embarrassed to be so rich.

Bread roll pun

The baker who was born in Bulawayo
looks at my rolls with a questioning eye.

I have to call out over the counter:
'Two white, two rye.'

Thoughts on emigration

One more hammock-bellied bureaucrat staggered to the buffet
and I started to imagine life in another country.

I subtracted the radio stations of America
from the silence of the virgin road to Sutherland.

I weighed the peaceful sheep of New Zealand
against the creak of my door swung open in the dark.

I foresaw our floating – too far from ropes
and the gentle knocking of familiar boats.

How to use a porcupine as an alibi

Sunday nights are spiritual occasions for my brother
he goes to church and comes home late and drunk
I mean, sometimes drunk.

One Monday morning following these wassails,
I noticed that the gate in the back yard was broken –
a chunk of masonry still clung to the wood.

And I said: 'Richard, did you break the gate last night?'
He did not answer me at first but only imperviously observed:
'On my way home I met a porcupine with shining eyes.
It looked at me *aggressively* in the dark.'

There was a pause while the word 'porcupine'
nosed its snuffling, feral way
into Monday morning's conversation.

Then I said: 'So are you saying that the porcupine broke the gate?'

I thought if I could get an admission from him,
we'd be one step closer to fixing the gate.

But we were way, way out now,
beyond the pale and gateless.

'I looked him in the eye,' he said (about the porcupine),
'and I thought: if you shoot me, I'll shoot you.'

My brother does not have a gun.

Way, way out, boundless,
beyond the pale and gateless.

This is the true story
of a standoff between man and beast in suburbia.

This is the true story
of how a half-blind, slow-moving rodent
caused a big-set, full-grown man to shoot our bolt.

This is the true story of the word 'porcupine'
and its triumph over the word 'gate'.

This is the true story of how to use a porcupine as an alibi
when explaining a broken gate to a poet.

I am the zebra

We each had to say who we were
and then it was the next girl's turn.

If this reminds you of life
then you're dead right.

'I am the *lion*,' claimed the tallest girl
in a reedy falsetto.

Somewhere on the Serengeti
a lion raised a shaggy brow
and showed his pride a skeptical tooth.

'I am the *elephant*,' admitted a plump girl
pinkly, with no hide at all.

Somewhere on the Serengeti
a war-torn elephant ear flapped
in irritation.

And so it went, down the row.

Parents strained to hear
the genteel *giraffe*, the civil *leopard*
the mild buffalo and, of course,
the unobtrusive rhinoceros.

I was the smallest –
sickness had put me off my food –
but I had the voice of a seventh child
and I knew what this was all about.

'I am the ZEBRA!' I called out.
I called out for the quagga, for the muzzled,
for all browsers, for the small, for the ungulate,
for the hunted, for the herd:
'I am the ZEBRA!'

And though the audience laughed
(such a small girl with such a big bark),
somewhere on the Serengeti
my courageous vegetarian kin
looked up, and nodded.

Summarising life

Summarising life is not easy.
My first try went like this:
You're born,
you go to the dentist,
then you die.

But that didn't quite capture all the pain,
so I tried again:
You're born,
you take your car to the mechanic,
then you die.

I was getting warmer,
I was definitely in the right room;
I just didn't know which cupboard life was in.

That's when I looked out of the window:
the full moon ran across the bay towards me
and Paderewski played Chopin on the TV.

So I wrote:
You're born, you hear the *Polonaise héroique*;
you forget the dentist and the mechanic,
then you die.

No, not quite. Try, try, try:

You die. You go to the dentist.
You take your car to the mechanic.
You look out of the window.

The full moon runs towards you across the sea.
Paderewski brings his hands down on the keys.

You're born; you start crying.
Eventually, you do die.

But the only part you're conscious of
– the only part that stays –
is the Polonaise.

Change Is Possible

(2014)

Micheál Mac Liammóir came to Cape Town in 1962

And so did I.

My mother dressed quickly and slipped past the nuns
to see him in *The Importance of Being Oscar*.

Recognising the importance of being alive,
I bawled for her milk-stained shirtfront.

Mrs Dowling! Gone to the theatre!
And your baby crying these last four hours!

Barely a mile from my not-nursing home,
a six-year-old boy tried – was tried – for flamboyant wit

in a home where you couldn't say 'gay',
or ask why Uncle Ivan shot himself in a hotel room,

or discuss Oscar Wilde
or any other parallel.

Later, these two lines crossed.

Ditty

I loved you so, so, so long ago
that the feeling has departed.
But not to worry, never mind:
I hate you still by heart.

Caveat

I'm sitting here listening to Bob Dylan,
trying to recall something Oscar Wilde said about disciples,
remembering my husband's dimples
and the long strong bones of his face
and his compact body – part-dancer, part-clown –

and how late one afternoon,
when he was still an acquaintance,
in his Volkswagen Beetle with its impatient dents,
his left hand came to rest on my knee
and for once I felt unafraid of sex and of learning to drive
(the two were inextricably connected in my mind).
I wanted his baby and a driving license immediately.

Other men might kill for such a recipe,
but he was in no hurry;
his hand on my knee as casual as a seal asleep
beneath the waves of laughter and after-laughter,
beneath the quotes and snatches of song,
beneath the mimicry and the Beetle's roar.

Nothing that I may say after this
and nothing you may privately think about biology,
in any way lessens the Volkswagen epiphany
or ends that afternoon.

Wanting to get divorced #1365

After the measles and whooping cough jabs
our daughter was restless and tearful
reaching screeching point on the baby rack.

You were looking forward to your vichyssoise
but I said bluntly, *We have to take her home*

In the dark car while she slept
with still-shuddering breath,
you told me that our baby,
at nine months old,
was selfish and wilful;
she had knowingly performed;
you resented her and the lack of soup;
you wanted your old life back.

You wondered whether you shouldn't
drop us in the dark driveway
and dine alone in some elegant, baby-free place.

I said: *Yes, go eat: go eat a lot.*
Try to fill the vacuum where your soul used to be.

Fifteen years later, thin and coughing
your once-deep voice now high and girlish
you asked: *Forgive me – I have done you wrong*
And I said: *There is nothing to forgive,*

because I don't want to forgive you.
I want you to come back as a mother.

How sweet the dead are now

How sweet the dead are now that they've stopped
sleeping around and wanting royalties and fame.

How dear the dead are now that they've given up
drinking so much and opening the door in their underpants.

How unvexing the dead are now that they pay their way
and only come when invited.

Next time you visit, remind me to play you
a few cuts from my boxed set of the dead.

Such a sweet sound, this turning round in graves.

I gossip with my sister about the future

Apparently, I say –
dropping my voice,
shielding the rest of the world from the news –
We're not just going to turn 50,
But 60, 70 and 80 too!

She is shocked.
Really? she asks, wide-eyed, amused.
We glut on the goriness of the rumour.

But by and by, for we are gentler than we seem,
we turn to higher things,
and relegate the rumour of old age
to where it belongs, alongside
other unbelievable scandals of fraud and bestiality.

On not liking oneself

I don't like my personality very much.
It's as if I picked it out in a hurry
in some trans-migratory vestibule of the soul

like a coat you might grab from a hook
as an afterthought, just as you're leaving,
because you don't know how cold it'll be where you going.

That's why I've arrived here in this singular,
rather prickly, buttoned-up duffel-jacket of a character

only to find that you are all apparently dressed
for a game of naked volleyball on the beach.

It's not that I want to join in:
I just want you to be curious.

The consolation of enmity

No need to lie awake at night
berating yourself for your character faults –
all the things you did and said wrong today.

Somewhere, someone else is doing that for you.

The quest

My friend travelled the world
in search of an answer.

In cherry-blossom season
he walked from Kyoto to Tokyo,
ate the fish that kills and lived.

In Kolkata he slept beside his swami
and recited at dawn
the one-thousand-and-four names of Lord Ram.

But it was in a Sandton car-tomb,
on a Johannesburg parking machine,
that the message he needed flashed through:

Change is possible, it said.

To adventurers, as far as I'm concerned

There is a climber on TV dangling
from a rope about to die.
He reminds me of the stranded balloonist
parched in the desert, about to die;
who reminds me of the solo yachtsman
with broken arms, 4000 kilometres from anywhere, about to die;
who reminds me of the men who tried to play
Scott-of-the-Antarctic, Scott-of-the-Antarctic
and who ended up hating each other, and about to die.

Oh misled, unfortunate adventurers: stay home!
What would it take to make you stay at home?
There's so much to do: Make tea! Clean out the shed!
Find your inner mountain and climb it.
Find your inner sea and chart it.
Find your inner arid plain and trudge across it,
as we all do, daily,
harnesses in the canyon
crampons in the glacier.

Imagine how much we'd save on search and rescue
if you would only stay at home.
Imagine how many we could save
if you would only cease this quest for accidental death
and talk about your feelings; or clean the shed.

Mise-en-abyme

I'm standing next to the microwave again,
waiting for the dog's gravy to get warm –
there's no brio here, nothing glam or bling:
I will stay here, breathing, till I hear the ping.

If you were outside looking in
you'd smile to see me through the iron bars
– portrait of the artist heating gravy –
– portrait of an artist staring

at a lighted cell she may not open
till the whirring stops and all goes dim.

Like you, I find it tiring, this tedium,
 all this Michael-Finnegan-begin-again

and yet: how urgently I want to be alive!
Dance, run, speak, hear, feel, write, sing!
I press my ear against tomorrow's ping.

Cupboards

She's weaned now, my daughter:
doesn't press me two-hourly
for heart-milk and breast-warmth anymore,
but I still demand to feed her.
                    What did you eat today?
And yesterday? What'll you eat tomorrow?
I'll make your favourite quiche on Friday.
Another girl at twenty might toss or sneer,
but mine volunteers:

Tuna, cheese, chicken, fried aubergine. Yes to the quiche.
On Sundays she leaves with sachets of pesto.
Blank spaces appear on my pantry shelves:
her theft thrills me.
                    It's another cupboard we're clearing,
twelve years on. We enter the listless, laughless room;
we reach behind the Disney t-shirts and, without blame
– small unopened packet by small unopened packet –
we feed the hungry child.

Authority

She's glad she didn't inherit my curly hair,
that I don't try to act young,
that I'd never join her at Happy Hour,
or make her a friend on Facebook,
or be on Facebook at all,
or gate-crash her parties.

She sighs when she has to help me with my phone,
or when I wear two pairs of sunglasses at the same time;
laughs when I ask *So what's this festival called*
 'Burn it all up in the Karoo'?

But when she sits by the kettle with her friend
and the two blonde heads talk in depth about life –
How do we heal things? How do we solve things?
Is this love? And who are we anyway? –
                              all I hear is:
My mum says my mum says my mum says my mum says

Composition

Two things I was thinking about this morning:
the one is that I want to write a poem about
not wanting to write a poem; not wanting anything.
It's hankering that makes us unhappy.

The other thing I was thinking about this morning
was *damn all this sunshine*.
Poets from the north write good poems
because they're always seeing things in the half light
of a chilly cathedral; poets from the north
are always having titanium-white epiphanies in the snow.

But each day around here dawns warm and cloudless,
and little pale green sea snails twirl on the sandy flats
of the low tide beach that stretches out before me
for as long as I want to walk.
It's unfair.

The abuse of cauliflowers

When I think of poetry scholars –
poetry academics –
I think of the way I make cauliflower soup –
how I hack at the white flowers,
how I toss them about in buttery onions and curry powder,
how I boil them in milk and vegetable stock
and then pound the whole lot up with a mechanical blender
and serve the resulting mess with stinky blue cheese.

I never dwell for a moment
on the cauliflower's pre-soup thoughts,
its pre-soup longings.
It's as if I don't care
how once this cauliflower lay in bed beside another cauliflower,
and the two of them made stock jokes, mocked celery,

and whispered, from the very bottom of their cauliflowerness,
about wanting to be loved for themselves.

The lawmaker

The lawmaker woke up in a free country
He smiled at girls chatting about their future in the sun
He rolled down his window and called for a newspaper
He laughed at the cartoon on page five
He joined the discussion round the coffee machine
He asked the web for an answer
He phoned the radio to say what was on his mind
He listened without fear to his son's hot, young ideas
He disagreed with his neighbour over the fence
He thanked his wife for twenty-five wonderful years
He stretched and looked up at the blue and unbarred sky
Then he went into his office and wrote the new law,
yawned, and flicked off the lights on a free country.

New Poems

Casting the cat and the bull

My sister took the dogs up the mountain:
Titch the cat waited for them on the high road.
Various dogs and humans (and time itself) passed by,
but Cara and the brother dogs did not return.

Titch's habits tipped out of Cara's mind.
She'd come home on the low road,
fed the dogs, poured a glass of wine:
Tigger on her lap, Rusty at her feet.

Meanwhile, all alone in the falling night, waited Titch.
Her eyes switched on in the steadfast pitch.
Titch had a conviction and she stayed fixed.
But Cara and the dogs did not pitch.

At last Cara remembered: Oh poor Titch!
She put down her glass and climbed the back steps. Sksskskss!
Out of the shadows grateful Titch ran to meet my sister
and the greeting-full dogs, and they all went home together.

I couldn't have told you a nicer story.
But there is also a grownup story.

                           *   *   *

Joseph sold his bull to a neighbour.
The bull was too small, and its calves too small,
so it had to have its throat slit.
The bull was penned in a new kraal
ahead of the feast and the slitting of its neck.

The bull remembered its old kraal,
its cows, calves and heifers, and Joseph, its human.
The bull broke out and ran to its remembered home.
It stood at Joseph's gate, bellowing to be let in.
But Joseph, though sore in his heart, was firm.

On butchering day, the bull would not submit.
Only Joseph might tie him to the tree;
Only Joseph might scratch his head between his horns;
It must be Joseph who places the halter around his neck
It must be Joseph who steadies him for the knife.

*   *   *

I am making these stories into a movie
and I need to cast all the parts:
the dogs, the cat, Cara, Joseph, and the bull.

I thought it would be hard to find a Titch,
but it turns out plenty cats like theatrics.

A lot of interest, of course, in the dog roles:
no more, please – I'm only taking two –
and, fingers crossed, Charlize Theron is considering the part of Cara.

So I have most of the actors I need.
But someone has to play the bull.

And someone, always, must be Joseph.

Unforgettable

A quarter of a century ago a woman said:
> *You have such a terrible voice.*
> *I don't know how your students can bear to listen to you.*

Such longevity has to be admired.
An insult like that is like uranium
– you can store it forever.

In fact, you have to store it forever.

Perhaps you want to know what happened to this critic?
As I understand it, she went on to marry a pig farmer.

I mean – a man who is an expert on pigs.

Life lesson

I wonder why, in such a crowded classroom,
one girl is set apart.
No one sits beside or behind her;
only a blank page before her.
She doesn't speak or put up her hand,
only looks at me as if to say, please understand.

The desk is small, but I squeeze in beside her:
> *Tell me what you want to write, I ask.*
> *Ek wil skryf*, she whispers,
> *oor die hond wat nie kan blaf nie,*
> *maar hy wil leer blaf.*

You teach for thirty years
sometimes you wonder what it is that you teach,
or if it can even be taught.
But then one day a nine-year-old explains it to you.

Come, little soul, let me teach you to bark
> *– Once upon a time there was a dog –*
and, after that, I will teach you to howl.

To young women, urging them not to become competent

Daughters, do not become competent,
try hard not to do things well.

Leave food in the fridge to spoil
and clothes to lie where they fall.

If you do one thing well
you'll end up doing them all.

Never be kind. It's not a profession.
Let someone who is not you babysit and visit the sick.

If you do one thing well
you'll end up doing them all.

Cook for yourself. When it comes to turkeys and ham,
plead ignorance or vegetarianism.

If you do one thing well
you'll end up doing them all.

Most workplaces, you'll find, thrive on disaster.
You won't be loved for doing things better, or faster.

If you do one thing well
you'll end up doing them all.

Daughters, don't ever reach for a broom
unless you're planning to fly.

To my sisters, on selling the old family home

If we ever sell this house
we should advertise it as self-cleaning
and point out the friendly cash machine at the door.

This house, the agent can say, comes complete with an invisible chef
who remembers and replicates your favourite meals
and fills the cake tins at regular intervals.

Whoever buys this house should know the poetry of Robert Frost,
keep a bed permanently made up for one who will return at last,
lost, in search of a lockless home.

                   Also, the new owners should sleep lightly
in case of a midnight cry from one of the upstairs rooms; in case
     of a knock.

Or we could take all of these features with us, and only sell them
     the bricks.

My therapist asks when it is that I cry

I cry on waking, I reply,
at dawn, and when changing sides at midnight.
At traffic lights,
or on sitting down to write
and on my morning walks
(blaming the cold air).

I cry at the news, reading
how one person has been kind to another
in Orlando or Beijing.

In conversations, some words have become unsafe.
Warmth, for example, and *rock*, go off like guns.
I have to cover my face with a scarf.

(What'll I do when summer comes?
Wear an apron, perhaps – or laugh?)

Porridge is fine though: *porridge* is good.
I taught myself the porridge defence at school.
Who could cry at *porridge*, small-self reasoned,
or feel anything at all extreme,
when looking at a bowl of oats grown cold
in a dish with a dragon rim?

Porridge, porridge, porridge.

Even now, it quarter-rhymes with courage.

Dog produces Monet forgery

My worst mood is no different from yours.
I am alone and I can't stop being alone.
I go upstairs looking for comfort
in an empty house.
I can't see clearly,
but I find the small dog
wagging on my window seat.
I kneel before him, and he licks my face

until I am ready to stand up and look in the mirror.
He is modest, waiting for me to give my opinion of his work.
I name it 'Depression Sunrise' and we go looking for his leash.

Catch of the day

My therapist shakes her head.
It's much more complex than that, she says.

Even if I begin hesitantly:
– It seems to me, I say –
mimicking her style of hypothesis,
dangling before her some tadpole of my own analysis –
I'm wrong again in this.

Life cannot be scooped up like a fish.

Afterwards she sees me out.
My car is parked beneath a gumtree
and I want to say:

It seems to me that what we are looking at here
is a white Toyota Corolla parked beneath a gumtree.

Just to have one moment with no ambiguity!
To feel – even once – that I'm right,
that I'm holding – however briefly – the thing that slips away.

Beneath the eucalyptus
my Toyota sleeps in peace

but it is not a fish.

No. It's much more complex than that.

Identity crisis 2016

This year I learned that other people know me
better than I know myself.
A faux estate agent called me 'Fiona' and then
as we became less close, 'Fi'.
A friend told me the reason I was sad was because
I'd chosen to live my life without warmth
and that I was going to be very, very unhappy if I moved
because I had been so very, very happy in that house.
Another said I couldn't move because actually
I was the house, splendid beneath the moon.
He stared up at it longingly while I sat beside him, human.
An acquaintance, a retired tennis racquet threader, stopped me to say
I would be raped at the place where I was going to:
'They will have a field day raping you,' he said, smacking his lips.
My dog stopped chasing seaweed and bit him. I liked that.
Someone based a character on me and put her in a radio play.
I sounded so boring I nodded off.
My closest male friend sent me some Japanese porn
in response to a query I had about female orgasm.
He thought the pictures were educational.
I defrosted a chest freezer
finding fossilised panini shards in the final glacier.
I lifted solid concrete and got covered in bruises moving things.
It crossed my mind that I could train the national rugby team.
When things got really bad, I re-read all of Jane Austen
and some invigorating books about death and loneliness,
which I will make required reading for the Springboks
(when I get the job).
Towards the end, I found the Dean of Law hiding in my office.
I made a cup of tea for her. 'Who are you?' she asked.
'Um,' I said, unable to sum myself up,
even under cross-examination.

Distant mirror

We found the perfect place to skateboard,
taking turns down the wide, sloping tar
as if we were grinding the surface
even finer for a faster ride.

But a woman appeared on the balcony above
and said 'Go away, children, go away.
My husband is writing a book;
it's a very *lo-ong* book.'

As we trudged home, and for years after that,
we mocked the lady's loftiness – 'a very *lo-ong* book' –
and her dud of a spoilsport husband,
hunkered down over his blank pages.

I look up from my keyboard and see her ghost
standing on the threshold of my life.
Oh long-book lady, listen to my woes:
Someone nearby is learning to play the drums,
and I have no wife.

It's only lunch

Here is the sandwich I have made for you, and the tea.
This sandwich does not mean:
'I will make you lunch in perpetuity.'
This cup of tea does not say:
'I want to lose my fingerprints through years of washing up your
cups.'

This is not tomorrow's sandwich, or tomorrow's cup of tea.
This lunch makes no covenant; it signs no treaty.
What you have is not a ticket.
You are eating two slices of bread joined with cheese.

I cannot even remember how you like your tea.

The problem with this game drawn out in chalk

Now that it's only a hop, skip and a jump
to the final square, I find that
my hip hurts, my knee twinges
and my toes grip the dust.

My mother the crocodile-tamer

Before he met my mother,
my father was engaged to a crocodile tamer
and snake charmer called Koringa.
One night over a bottle of wine
we wondered what we'd have been like
if our mother had been a crocodile tamer
or a snake charmer, 'the only female fakir
in the world'. We watched a YouTube clip of Koringa
putting her head into a crocodile's mouth
and swinging snakes around
while a man sounding a bit like my father
did a BBC-type narration in the background.
Koringa wore a miniskirt and a tasselled bra
and her hair stood out like a fan.
It took £600 and three Rosminians to stop her
at the church door.
                    We'd have been there too,
if we could. When night fell, our mother closed the curtains;
our mother read us to sleep in a warm voice;
our mother didn't go larking about with reptiles.

Party invitations

My classmates were invited to a party.
They showed me the invitation:
princesses arriving at a palace.
I told my father:
there is this party at a palace
and I'm not invited.

My father phoned Mrs Osbourne and said:
'My daughter is very sad to be left out.'
Mrs Osbourne said 'Oh dear, then let her come,'
even though I never spoke, or played with anyone.

          We pulled up at the wrong address.
The party girl was there, yes,
and her friends with invitations,
but they did not look like princesses and
behind the picket fence,
no palace but a bungalow.

I've been invited to a party next week.
The invitation shows people in evening dress
drinking and playing jazz instruments on the roof.

I just don't know how I'm going to get up there.

Why I love an insult

You're not at the bottom,
– I mean, you're at least one rung above.
Your poetry is very gossipy.
You're not an intellectual.
Your hair is falling out in chunks,
–and you didn't have very much to start off with.
I can't believe so many people want to attend your lecture.
I'd forgotten how short you are.
When you walked into the room,
I really wasn't expecting anything.

I like an insult,
the way it fits into my palm
like a hand grenade
or my own Marmite jar.

I don't *want* it but
I *know* it; it has a place:
my hand closes over it;
it fits.

Watch out.

Unhappiness

is just the gap between what I want –
the stone hut on the mountain,
nothing but birdsong
and the cry of the wild baboon,
and you, with that look in your eye
like you're going to make a road
where there's never been a road;
like you're going after the source.

That is what I want. What I have is
a queue of people wanting their money back
because the lecture on women in physics was 'boring'.

But I also have an assistant
who is telling the unhappy crowd:
'We only give refunds on medical grounds,
and as far as I'm aware
boredom is not a medical condition.'

I also have a memory of you
parting the branches,
clearing the mulched leaves,
and saying: 'See, this is the source.'

Two bodies could not be less alike than ours

You stoop to enter a room.
I climb onto a chair to put away a plate.

Your blood pressure before medication is 180/100.
My doctor says, 'You're barely here.'

I bruise on wooden table corners.
You opt for your eighth arthoscopy.

I imagine a snow cave, and I fall asleep.
You lie awake reciting *The Song of Wandering Aengus*

in your head, in another city, beside your wife.

One in a million

Although otherwise a humble man
Pete tells me he is one in a million.

all because
        a single sperm,
one of the 276.25 million
        ejaculated by his father that night,
one of the 525 billion
        ejaculated by his father
in a lifetime of ejaculation
        (though he was apparently a quiet man,
a collector of birds' eggs),
        this container of Pete's Pete-ness
against the odds
        wiggled its singular way to the front
to the egg-in-waiting
        on or about
thirteenth January 1945.

It wasn't likely,
but it happened.
Pete was the lucky one, he says.
He was incarnated;
he got to meet me –
all because of a gold medal sperm.

I said that's very nice, Pete,
that's very romantic.
Well done.
Thank you for your effort.

But remember the egg, Pete,
remember the egg.

When panicking, think of the recently dead

My mouth is dry
my eyes are dry
I grind my teeth
I clench my jaw
my scalp is itchy

words won't stay still on the page
terrible things are happening in my dreams
every now and then the world completely de-realises itself
and I stand holding a clothes peg
which is as incomprehensible as the Higgs-Boson to me

I put lavender oil on my forehead
I take magnesium and Vitamin B
I close my bedroom door
I get into bed before sunset
I switch off my phone
I take a tranquilliser

I am scared of Monday to Friday
and Saturday and Sunday too.

Then I see that Christine Keeler is dead
Johnny Hallyday is dead:

They have completed the tax return of life.
My God, they don't even have to exercise
where they are!

No meetings
no calendars, no auto out-of-office replies,
just lots of spirits.

Oh happy, happy Hallyday; happy Keeler
I'm going to lie in bed and drink and pretend to be you.

Doubt

When there's no reply, I don't ask:
'Why is there no reply?'
because silence itself is a quiet reply,
and more than one silence is a chorus.

'Doubt! Doubt!' it calls out,
until doubt wobbles in through a chink,
flitters anxiously across the room,
like this fruit fly to my whiskey glass.

When I am in doubt
I am as unsteady as a fruit fly,
dying to drown
down in the drink
I have already poured for it.

Cheers!

Ilk

I am reading with my usual careless fluency
when the word 'ilk' stops me
in the most unlikely way.
I know 'ilk', of course,
as a way of casting off unlikeable types –
tow-truck drivers and their ilk –
but not what ilk might have meant, once,
to women wearing bearskins.

How can I read on when the page holds
a word so robust it has outrun
the cosy *pantofle* and the useful *vomitorium*?
Ilk, I bow before you. You are sturdy
as a three-legged milking stool
passed from ilk to ilk, like to like
for more than a thousand years,
and the cause here of my pause
to make the unlikely likely.

How a house feels when we leave

I wonder how a house feels when we leave.
Does it wait at the window like a dog,
ears hinged to the horizon, herald of
every gate squeak, every brake pull?

And if we travel far, does a house feel
like a child on her first day at a foreign school
lying awake at nap-time, eyes turned to the doorframe
willing the known one to appear?

And if we never come back, does a house feel as empty
as a lover who must hear her song sung to another?

No. I think

the naked house thrills to the touch of the new hand,
practises all the words of the new tongue,
starting, perhaps, with 'Welcome.'

ACKNOWLEDGEMENTS

This selection is drawn from the collections *I flying* (Carapace, 2002); *Doo-Wop Girls of the Universe* (Penguin, 2006); *Notes from the Dementia Ward* (Kwela, 2008) and *Change Is Possible* (Poetry Trust, 2014). Some poems in the New Poems section have previously appeared in *Illuminations, New Contrast* and *The North.*

The poem 'Loving Novels' which appears here is a shortened version of the original in *Doo-Wop Girls of the Universe.*

I would like to thank Naomi Jaffa for inviting me to read for The Poetry Trust at Aldeburgh Poetry Festival in 2014, setting off a chain of events that has resulted in the publication of this book.